Georgia, My State
Rivers

Chattahoochee River

by Diane Carr

Your State • Your Standards • Your Grade Level

Dear Educators, Librarians and Parents . . .

Thank you for choosing the *"Georgia, My State"* Series! We have designed this series to support the Georgia Department of Education's Georgia Performance Standards for elementary level Georgia studies. Each book in the series has been written at appropriate grade level as measured by the ATOS Readability Formula for Books (Accelerated Reader), the Lexile Framework for Reading, and the Fountas & Pinnell Benchmark Assessment System for Guided Reading. Photographs and/or illustrations, captions, and other design elements have been included to provide supportive visual messaging to enhance text comprehension. Glossary and Word Index sections introduce key new words and help young readers develop skills in locating and combining information.

We wish you all success in using the *"Georgia, My State"* Series to meet your student or child's learning needs. For additional sources of information, see www.georgiaencyclopedia.org.

Jill Ward, President

Publisher
State Standards Publishing, LLC
1788 Quail Hollow
Hamilton, GA 31811
USA
1.866.740.3056
www.statestandardspublishing.com

Library of Congress Cataloging-in-Publication Data
Carr, Diane, 1955-
  Chattahoochee River / by Diane Carr.
      p. cm. -- (Georgia, my state. Rivers)
  Includes index.
  ISBN-13: 978-1-935077-54-1 (hardcover)
  ISBN-10: 1-935077-54-6 (hardcover)
  ISBN-13: 978-1-935077-61-9 (pbk.)
  ISBN-10: 1-935077-61-9 (pbk.)
  1. Chattahoochee River--Description and travel--Juvenile literature. I. Title.
  F292.C4C37 2009
  975.8--dc22
                              2009036396

Copyright © 2010 by State Standards Publishing, LLC. All rights reserved. No part of this book may be reproduced, stored, or transmitted in any form or by any means without prior written permission from the publisher.

Printed in the United States of America, North Mankato, Minnesota, October 2009, 070209.

About the Author

Diane Carr has a master's degree in middle grades education from Columbus State University in Columbus, Georgia and currently shares her love of learning with her 7th-grade science students in Harris County, Georgia. Besides learning and teaching, she enjoys photography, camping, and reading and has been a frequent photographic contributor to the *Georgia, My State* series books. She resides in Columbus, Georgia with her husband, Robin.

Table of Contents

Let's Explore! 5
Recreation on the River 7
An Important Reservoir 9
Dams Changed the River 11
Clean the Wastewater 13
A Pollution Problem 15
The River Slows Down 17
Problems Sharing the Water 19
Lakes and Locks 21
Glossary 22
Word Index .23
Georgia Map 24

The Chattahoochee starts as a small stream.

Let's Explore!

Hi, I'm Bagster! Let's explore the Chattahoochee River! The Chattahoochee is important to people in north and west Georgia. The **headwaters** of the river are high in the Blue Ridge Mountains. This is where it starts. Water bubbles up out of the ground. This is called a **spring**. It is a very small river when it is in the mountains.

People tube on the river.

People fish for trout.

Rapids churn the water.

Recreation on the River

The river tumbles down the mountain. Streams join the river. It grows bigger. **Rapids** churn the water. Rapids are waters that move fast. Trout swim in the clear, cold stream. People fish for trout and ride tubes on the Chattahoochee. Would you rather tube or fish?

Trout

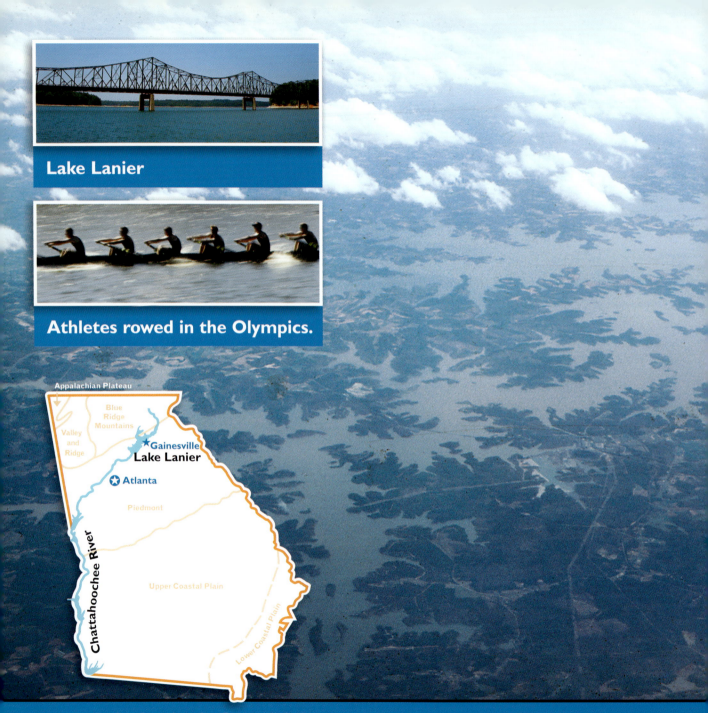

Lake Lanier

Athletes rowed in the Olympics.

Lake Lanier is Georgia's largest lake.

An Important Reservoir

The Chattahoochee River leaves the mountains. It flows into Lake Lanier at Gainesville. Lake Lanier is a **reservoir**. It holds water for Atlanta. Lake Lanier is Georgia's largest lake. Athletes rowed boats here in the 1996 **Olympic Games**. They came from all over the world to take part in this sports competition.

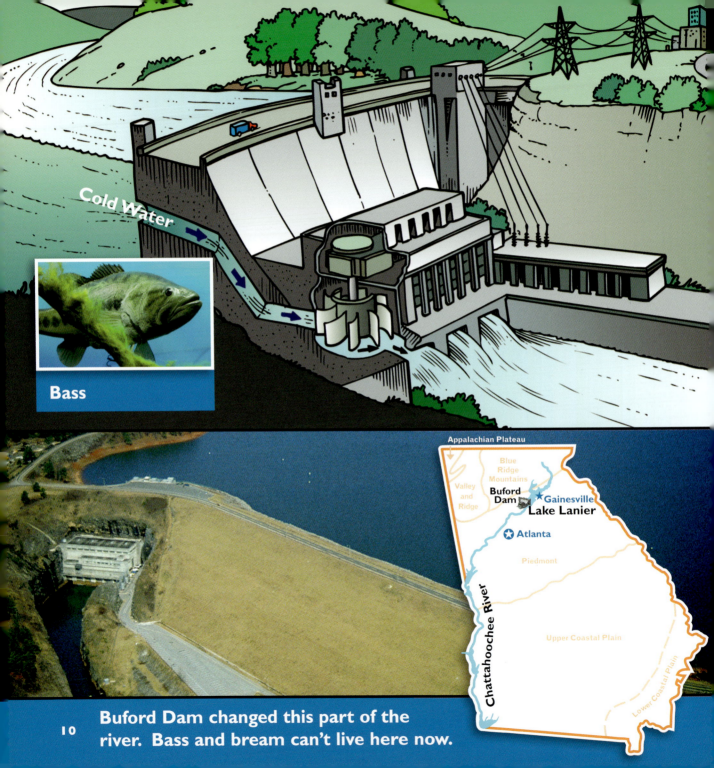

Buford Dam changed this part of the river. Bass and bream can't live here now.

Dams Changed the River

There are thirteen **dams** on the Chattahoochee! Dams block the river. They make electricity and form lakes. Some lakes are deep and cold. Buford Dam makes Lake Lanier. The water was once warm below the lake. Bass and bream lived in the warm water. Buford Dam has made the water colder. Now, trout live here instead.

Bream

People use water in their toilets.

People use water to wash dishes.

Clean the Wastewater

People use water to bathe and wash dishes. They use water in their toilets. Dirty water goes down the drain. It is called **wastewater**. Cities clean their wastewater. The clean water is put back in the river.

Cities put clean wastewater in the river.

Dirty wastewater pollutes the river.

Fish can't live in polluted water.

Many people live in Atlanta.

A Pollution Problem

There are many people in Atlanta. They make a lot of wastewater. The city cannot clean it all. The dirty water **pollutes** the Chattahoochee. It makes the river dirty. Fish cannot live where the water is too dirty. People cannot swim. Atlanta pays fines for polluting the Chattahoochee. They are trying to solve the problem.

You can see mounds the Indians built.

The river twists and turns like an S.

The Chattahoochee flows to Columbus.

The River Slows Down

The river forms the border between Georgia and Alabama. It flows to LaGrange and Columbus. It tumbles over the **fall line**. This is an area of land that falls steeply. Then, the river slows down. It twists and turns like an *S*. It warms up. Indians lived by the river 1,000 years ago. You can see **mounds** they built to bury their chiefs.

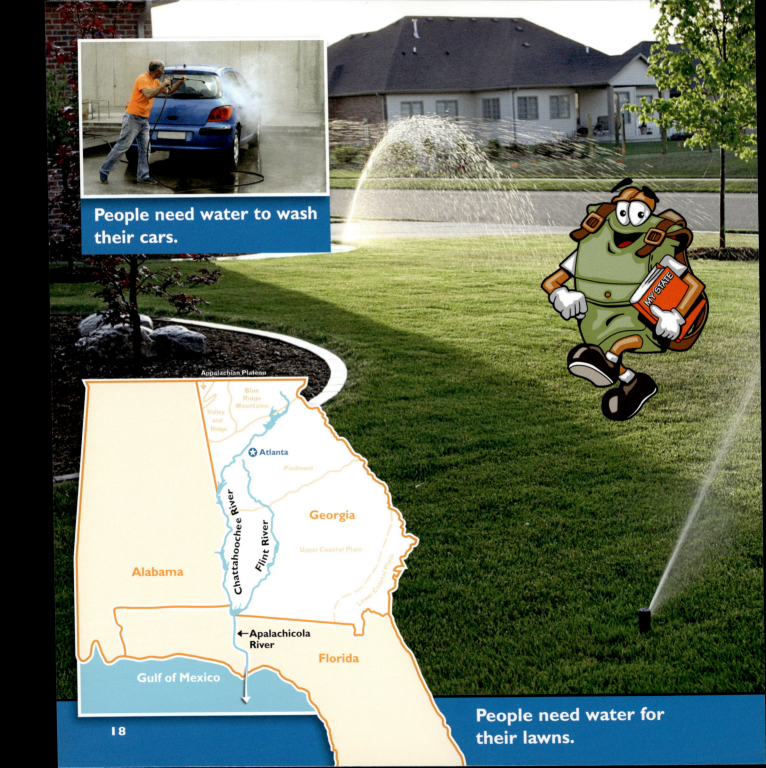

People need water to wash their cars.

People need water for their lawns.

18

Problems Sharing the Water

The Chattahoochee joins the Flint River in the Coastal Plain. The two rivers form the Apalachicola River in Florida. It takes Georgia's water to the Gulf of Mexico. People in Georgia need the water. People in Alabama and Florida need water, too. They cannot agree on how to share the water from Georgia.

People need water to drink.

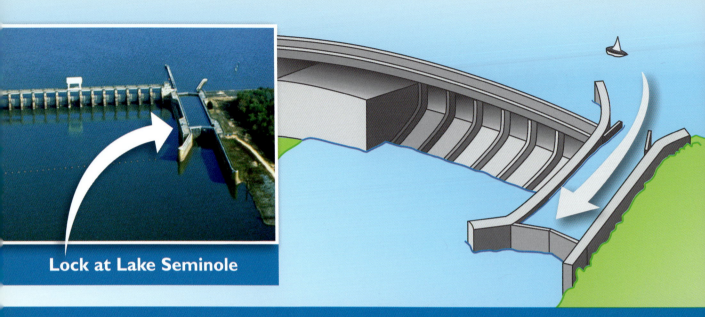

Lock at Lake Seminole

A boat goes into the lock at lake level.

It comes out at river level.

Lakes and Locks

Dams on the river make big lakes. West Point Lake and Lake Harding are here. Lake Walter F. George and Lake Seminole are here. Some of the lakes have **locks** on them. The locks act like elevators for boats. Water goes up and down in the locks. The boats go up and down, too. They let boats go from Columbus to the ocean!

Glossary

dams – Structures that block rivers to make electricity and form lakes.

fall line – An area of land that falls steeply.

headwaters – Small creeks and streams that become rivers.

locks – Structures in dams that level the water. Locks allow boats to travel up and down a river.

mounds – Places where Indian tribes buried their chiefs.

Olympic Games – A sports competition that athletes from all over the world compete in. The 1996 Olympic Games were held in Georgia.

pollutes – Makes dirty. Dirty wastewater pollutes rivers.

rapids – Water in a creek, stream, or river that moves fast.

reservoir – A lake that holds water to be used by towns and cities.

spring – Water under the ground that bubbles up to the surface.

wastewater – Water used by cities that is cleaned and put back in a river.

Word Index

Alabama, 17, 19
Apalachicola River, 19
Atlanta, 9, 15
bass, 11
Blue Ridge Mountains, 5
bream, 11
Buford Dam, 11
Coastal Plain, 19
Columbus, 17, 21
dams, 11, 21
electricity, 11

fall line, 17
Flint River, 19
Florida, 19
Gainesville, 9
Gulf of Mexico, 19
headwaters, 5
Indians, 17
LaGrange, 17
Lake Harding, 21
Lake Lanier, 9, 11
Lake Seminole, 21

Lake Walter F. George, 21
locks, 21
mounds, 17
Olympic Games, 9
pollutes, 15
rapids, 7
reservoir, 9
spring, 5
trout, 7, 11
wastewater, 13
West Point Lake, 21

Image Credits

p. 4 Headwaters: © Alan Cressler, Flickr.com
p. 6 Rapids: Photo courtesy of Georgia Department of Economic Development; Tubing: © Diane Carr, Columbus, Georgia; Fishing: © Oksana Perkins, fotolia.com
p. 7 Trout: © Richard Gunion, iStockphoto.com
p. 8 Lake Lanier: Photo courtesy of Ed Jackson, Carl Vinson Institute of Government, University of Georgia, Athens, Georgia; Bridge over Lake Lanier: Photo courtesy of Georgia Department of Economic Development; Rowers: © Gergo Orban, iStockphoto.com
p. 10 Dam: © Milorad Zaric, iStockphoto.com; Bass: © Dieter Spears, iStockphoto.com; Buford Dam: Photo courtesy of U. S. Army Corps of Engineers
p. 11 Bream: © Jay Adkins, iStockphoto.com
p. 12 Dish washing: © Oscar Williams, fotolia.com; Toilet: © Sarah Musselman, iStockphoto.com
p. 13 Wastewater: © Diane Carr, Columbus, Georgia
p. 14 Atlanta: Photo courtesy of Georgia Department of Economic Development; Wastewater: © Diane Carr, Columbus, Georgia; Fish: © Diane Carr, Columbus, Georgia
p. 16 All Photos: Photo courtesy of Georgia Department of Economic Development
p. 18 Lawn Watering: © Frances Twitty, iStockphoto.com; Car Washing: © Blade Kostas, iStockphoto.com
p. 19 Drinking: © Rob Friedman, iStockphoto.com
p. 20 Lock: Illustration courtesy of Michael Sellner, Corporate Graphics, North Mankato, Minnesota; Lake Seminole Lock: Photo courtesy of U. S. Army Corps of Engineers

Georgia, My State Rivers

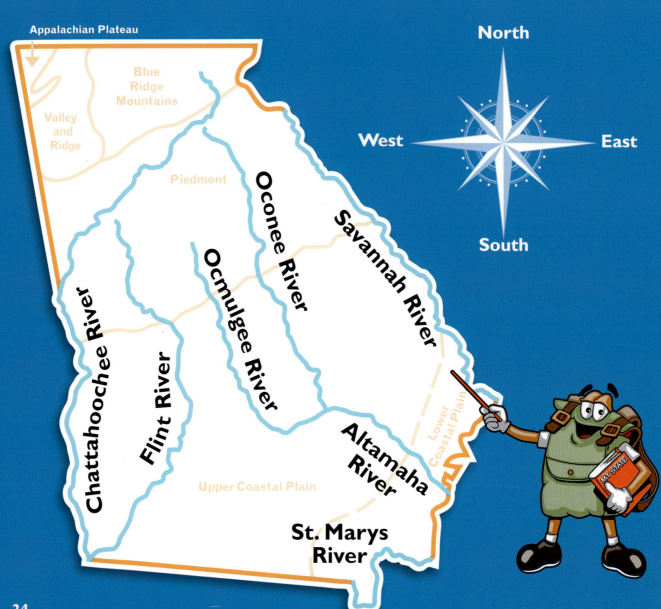